Table of Contents

INTRODUCTION	2
CHAPTER 1: THE FOUNDATIONS OF MARKETING PSYCHOLOGY	5
CHAPTER 2: PERCEPTION AND ATTENTION IN MARKETING	6
CHAPTER 3: MOTIVATION AND DECISION-MAKING	8
CHAPTER 4: THE PSYCHOLOGY OF BRANDING AND IDENTITY	10
CHAPTER 5: SOCIAL INFLUENCE AND PERSUASION TECHNIQUES	12
CHAPTER 6: EMOTION-DRIVEN MARKETING	14
CHAPTER 7: THE ROLE OF CONSUMER PSYCHOLOGY IN DIGITAL MARKETING	16
CHAPTER 8: NEUROMARKETING AND THE SCIENCE OF BUYING BEHAVIOR	19
CHAPTER 9: PRICING PSYCHOLOGY	21
CHAPTER 10: CONSUMER JOURNEY MAPPING AND TOUCHPOINTS	23
CHAPTER 11: BEHAVIORAL ECONOMICS AND CHOICE ARCHITECTURE	26
CHAPTER 12: LONG-TERM CUSTOMER RELATIONSHIPS AND RETENTION	29
CHAPTER 13: ETHICS IN MARKETING PSYCHOLOGY	32

CHAPTER 14: FUTURE TRENDS IN MARKETING PSYCHOLOGY   35

CONCLUSION   38

Marketing Psychology Q&A

by

Pinnacle Press

Introduction

In today's competitive world, understanding why people buy things is important for brands. This goes beyond focusing on prices or product details. Marketing psychology looks at emotions, thoughts, and social influences that guide decisions, often made without much logic.

With so many messages and choices around, grabbing attention and connecting with people emotionally is key. This book explains how brands can use psychology to communicate better, keep customers loyal, and increase sales. It covers ideas like how people see things, feel, and react, as well as newer methods like studying brain activity and decision-making behavior.

As people's preferences keep changing, learning these psychological principles can help brands create strong connections, build trust, and succeed. This book is a guide to using these ideas effectively in marketing.

Chapter 1: The Foundations of Marketing Psychology

1. What is marketing psychology?

Marketing psychology is about understanding how people think and behave when they see ads or products. It helps businesses connect with customers in ways that feel natural and appealing.

2. Why does marketing psychology matter?

It helps businesses grab attention and build trust with customers. Knowing how people make choices makes it easier to sell products and create loyal customers.

3. How do ideas like "social proof" and "scarcity" help in marketing?

"Social proof" shows people what others like, such as reviews. "Scarcity" makes things feel special by showing they're limited. Both encourage people to buy more confidently and quickly.

4. Why are emotions important in marketing?

People often buy based on feelings, like happiness or nostalgia. Ads that make us feel good or remind us of nice memories make products more attractive.

5. Can small businesses use marketing psychology too?

Yes! Even simple things, like asking for reviews or creating special offers, can make a big difference without spending much money.

Chapter 2: Perception and Attention in Marketing

1. Why do some ads grab attention while others don't?

Ads stand out when they use bold colors, surprising images, or moving elements like videos. People also notice ads that match their interests or needs.

2. What tricks do ads use to get noticed?

Ads use things like bright colors, unexpected ideas, faces, and animations. These grab our attention quickly and make us curious.

3. How does color affect how we see a brand?

Colors make us feel certain ways. For example, blue feels trustworthy, red feels exciting, and green feels natural. Picking the right color helps a brand send the right message.

4. Can you give examples of how colors are used?

Fast-food places often use red and yellow to make us hungry. Luxury brands use black or gold to feel fancy, while eco-friendly brands use green to feel natural.

5. Why do we remember some brands but not others?

We remember brands that are simple, consistent, and make us feel something. Using the same logo, colors, and message over time helps people recall them.

6. How can brands help people remember them?

Brands can stick to a look and message, use catchy songs or slogans, and show ads that make people laugh or feel inspired.

7. How do fonts and layouts affect how we see a brand?

Fonts tell a story, fancy fonts feel elegant, while plain ones feel modern. A good layout makes ads easy to read and helps people find the important stuff, like buttons to click.

8. Why do visuals matter in ads?

Pictures grab attention faster than words. Smiling faces feel friendly, and cool designs feel innovative. A consistent look helps people recognize a brand easily.

9. What is sensory marketing, and why does it work?

Sensory marketing uses smells, sounds, or textures to make people notice and remember a brand. More senses mean stronger memories.

10. Can you share examples of sensory marketing?

Coffee shops use the smell of coffee to draw you in. Stores play music to make shopping fun. Fancy brands use nice packaging to feel high-end.

Chapter 3: Motivation and Decision-Making

1. Why do people decide to buy certain things?

People buy things because of needs (like food or safety) or desires (like feeling special or successful). A mix of both often drives decisions.

2. How can brands know what people want?

Brands can ask customers directly, check social media, or look at buying habits to learn what people need or want.

3. What's the difference between needs and desires?

Needs are basics, like a warm jacket in winter. Desires are extras, like a designer coat that looks stylish.

4. How do brands appeal to both?

A brand might say their product works well for everyday needs and also makes life more enjoyable or exciting.

5.a. What are cognitive biases?

Cognitive biases are shortcuts our brain uses to make decisions. Sometimes they lead us to think in certain ways without realizing it.

5.b. Can you share examples of these biases?

Anchoring: If something costs $100 but is on sale for $50, the sale feels like a big deal.

Loss Aversion: We hate losing more than we love gaining, so we rush to buy limited offers.
Confirmation Bias: We like things that match what we already believe.

6. Why do "limited-time offers" work so well?

When something feels rare or urgent, we think it's more valuable and act fast to avoid missing out.

7. How can brands use this without being pushy?

Brands should be honest. They can offer real limited-time deals, seasonal sales, or special releases without faking scarcity.

8. Why do people sometimes regret buying things?

Regret happens when a product doesn't meet expectations or feels like a rushed decision.

9. How can brands reduce regret?

Brands can:

Be clear about what the product can do.
Offer easy returns or guarantees.
Check in with customers to make sure they're happy.
Remind buyers of the good reasons they chose the product.

Chapter 4: The Psychology of Branding and Identity

1. Why do people feel connected to some brands?

People connect with brands that share their values or make them feel understood. For example, someone who cares about the environment may love a brand that promotes eco-friendly products.

2. How does a brand's personality help make connections?

A brand's personality makes it feel human. Fun brands attract playful people, while professional brands appeal to those who prefer tradition and reliability.

3. How do brands build trust?

Trust comes from keeping promises, being honest, and staying consistent. A brand that listens to its customers and communicates openly is more likely to be trusted.

4. What makes a brand relatable?

A brand feels relatable when it shows it understands its customers, uses friendly language, and even shares personal stories or admits mistakes.

5. Why do shared values matter for loyalty?

When a brand reflects a customer's values, it feels like they're on the same team. This shared connection keeps customers coming back.

6. How does personality help with loyalty?

A consistent brand personality feels familiar, like a reliable friend. Customers stick with brands they trust and feel comfortable with.

7. Why is storytelling important for brands?

Stories make brands more memorable and relatable. A good story about a brand's journey or mission can inspire emotions and create a deeper connection.

8. What makes a brand story effective?

A great story includes relatable people, challenges the brand overcame, its purpose or values, and emotions that stick with the audience.

9. How does a brand's identity affect loyalty?

A strong brand identity, like a clear logo, colors, and values, makes it easy for customers to recognize and trust the brand, leading to loyalty.

10. Why do loyal customers promote brands to others?

When a brand's identity aligns with a customer's values and personality, they feel proud to share it. Familiar and trustworthy brands are easy to recommend.

Chapter 5: Social Influence and Persuasion Techniques

1. What is social proof, and why is it important?

Social proof is when people look at others' choices to guide their own decisions. If a product has great reviews or is popular, people are more likely to trust and buy it.

2. How can brands use social proof?

Brands can show customer reviews, share testimonials, highlight best-sellers, or use influencers to recommend their products.

3. Why do people trust reviews more than ads?

Reviews come from real customers, so they feel honest and unbiased. Ads are made by the brand, so they feel less personal.

4. How can brands get more reviews?

Brands can ask customers directly, offer discounts for leaving reviews, or make the review process simple.

5.a. What is the foot-in-the-door technique?

The foot-in-the-door technique is when you ask someone for a small action first, like signing up for a newsletter, before asking for a bigger action, like buying something.

5.b. Can you give an example?

A brand might offer a free trial, and once the trial ends, ask the customer to subscribe for full access.

6. How does authority build trust in marketing?

People trust experts, so when a product is recommended by an authority figure, like a doctor or a trusted professional, it feels more reliable.

7. How can brands show authority?

Brands can display certifications, share expert endorsements, or publish research that supports their product's quality.

8. What tricks make marketing messages persuasive?

Reciprocity: Giving something free, like a sample, makes people feel like giving back.
Scarcity: Saying "only a few left" makes people act quickly.
Consistency: Starting with a small action leads to bigger commitments.
Framing: Phrasing things positively, like "Save 20%" instead of "Don't lose 20%."

9. How can brands use these tricks fairly?

Brands can use these tricks fairly by being honest. Only creating urgency when it's real and always focusing on giving true value to customers. This builds trust, not pressure.

Chapter 6: Emotion-Driven Marketing

1. Why are emotions so important in marketing?

People often decide to buy based on feelings first, then use logic to justify it. Emotional ads grab attention, stick in memory, and build connections with customers.

2. What emotions do brands use most often?

Brands use happiness, nostalgia, excitement, and fear. Happiness makes people feel good and share things. Nostalgia brings back fond memories. Excitement creates buzz, and fear encourages quick action, especially for safety or health products.

3. How does joy affect buying?

Joy makes people more likely to try, share, and buy. Ads that make people laugh or feel happy create a positive link to the brand.

4. How is fear used in marketing?

Fear motivates action by highlighting risks, like not having insurance. But it works best when paired with a solution to reassure people.

5. What about nostalgia or sadness in marketing?

Nostalgia connects with happy memories, building trust and loyalty. Sadness can create a strong emotional bond, especially in heartfelt or meaningful campaigns.

6. Why do stories make ads more emotional?

Stories make brands relatable by showing real struggles, triumphs, or values. A good story with characters, challenges, and a purpose makes people care about the brand.

7. What makes a story emotionally powerful?

A great story has relatable characters, a problem to solve, real emotions, and a message that reflects the brand's values. For example, an athlete's journey to success can inspire and connect with customers.

8. How does empathy help brands connect with customers?

Empathy shows customers that a brand understands their needs and cares about their experiences. This builds trust and loyalty.

9. Can you give an example of empathy in marketing?

During hard times, like a natural disaster, brands offering help like donations, flexible payments, or kind messaging show empathy and care for their customers.

10. How can brands use emotions without being manipulative?

Responsible marketing uses emotions to build trust and connection, not to pressure or mislead. For example, it's fine to show a problem if you also offer a real solution.

11. What's the key to ethical emotional marketing?

Brands should be honest, transparent, and focus on providing real value. This creates long-term trust instead of short-term pressure.

Chapter 7: The Role of Consumer Psychology in Digital Marketing

1. How is online shopping different from in-store shopping?

Online shopping is convenient and offers more choices but doesn't let you touch or try products. Shoppers rely on pictures, descriptions, and reviews instead of their senses.

2. What challenges do people face when shopping online?

Too many options can make decisions harder, and not being able to see or feel products can lead to doubts. Clear pictures, descriptions, and easy return policies help solve these problems.

3. Why are visuals so important for online shopping?

Since you can't touch or try items online, good visuals help you imagine how products will look and feel. High-quality pictures and videos make items more appealing.

4. How does website design affect shopping?

A good design makes it easy to find what you need, shop quickly, and check out without frustration. Clear menus, fast loading, and easy-to-use buttons keep shoppers happy.

5. Why do people like personalized recommendations?

Personalization makes shopping easier and feels special. It saves time by showing items that match your tastes, making you feel understood by the brand.

6. How do brands personalize recommendations?

Brands use data like past purchases or browsing history to suggest similar products. For example, if you buy a book, they might recommend another by the same author.

7. What is FOMO, and how does it work online?

FOMO, or Fear of Missing Out, makes people act fast to avoid losing something, like a sale or limited stock. Messages like "Only 2 left!" create urgency.

8. What other tactics do brands use online?

Brands use:

Social proof: Showing reviews or popular items to build trust.
Gamification: Reward systems like points or challenges.
Notifications: Reminders about cart items or new deals.
Countdowns: Timers for limited offers to speed up decisions.

9. How does psychology influence social media content?

Social media content works best when it grabs attention quickly and connects emotionally. Fun, helpful, or inspiring posts make people engage more.

10. What types of posts work well on social media?

Posts that work well include:

Behind-the-scenes: Showing real people behind the brand.
Educational content: Tips and how-tos.
User content: Sharing customer photos or reviews.
Interactive posts: Polls or quizzes that encourage participation.

These posts make brands relatable and fun to follow.

Chapter 8: Neuromarketing and the Science of Buying Behavior

1. What is neuromarketing?

Neuromarketing studies how the brain reacts to ads, logos, and packaging. It uses tools like brain scans and eye-tracking to learn what grabs attention and makes products appealing.

2. How is neuromarketing used in marketing?

Neuromarketing helps brands test things like ads and packaging before launching them. For example, they can see which colors or images make people feel excited or interested.

3.a. How does the brain influence buying decisions?

Different parts of the brain play a role in buying decisions:

The amygdala handles emotions like joy or fear.
The prefrontal cortex helps with logical thinking.
The nucleus accumbens lights up when we feel rewarded, like seeing a great deal.

3.b. How do these insights improve ads?

Marketers can use emotional words and images to make ads more memorable. Combining excitement with clear benefits helps create a stronger connection.

4. Is there a "buy button" in the brain?

Not exactly, but areas like the nucleus accumbens and orbitofrontal cortex influence feelings of reward and value, making people more likely to buy.

5.a. How does neuroscience help create better campaigns?

Neuroscience informs strategies like:

Eye-tracking: Ensuring important details catch attention first.
Emotional content: Using stories or visuals that invoke strong feelings.
Repetition: Reinforcing brand familiarity through repeated exposure.

5.b. Can you give an example?

Coca-Cola uses neuromarketing to refine its branding, ensuring its red color and iconic font invoke happiness and nostalgia in ads.

6. Why are ethics important in neuromarketing?

Neuromarketing taps into subconscious reactions, so there's a risk of unfair manipulation. Ethical practices ensure brands use insights to improve experiences, not exploit vulnerabilities.

7. How can brands practice ethical neuromarketing?

Brands can practice ethical neuromarketing by:

Being transparent about how data is used.
Using insights to make products or ads genuinely helpful.
Avoiding tactics that create unnecessary pressure or anxiety.

This builds trust and long-term customer relationships.

Chapter 9: Pricing Psychology

1. What is price framing, and how does it work?

Price framing shows prices in ways that make them look better. For example, showing the original price crossed out next to a discount makes the new price feel like a better deal.

2. What are some examples of price framing?

Discounts: Highlighting savings, like "Was $50, now $30."
Bundles: Offering packages at a lower combined price, like "Buy 2, Save 20%."
Small payments: Saying "$1 per day" instead of $365 per year.

3. Why do prices like $9.99 work better than $10?

Prices ending in .99 or .95 seem smaller because people focus on the first number. So, $9.99 feels closer to $9 than $10, even though the difference is tiny.

4. Does charm pricing work for everything?

Charm pricing is great for affordable products, but luxury brands often use whole numbers, like $100, to feel more premium.

5. What is loss aversion, and how does it affect pricing?

Loss aversion means people fear losing something more than they enjoy gaining. For example, saying, "Sale ends today!" makes people act fast to avoid missing out.

6. How does anchoring affect pricing?

Anchoring sets a comparison point, like showing a higher original price next to a discount. This makes the lower price feel like a great deal.

7. Why do discounts, bundles, and free offers work so well?

Let us understand why they work so well:

Discounts: Make people feel rewarded for saving money.
Bundles: Create value by offering more for less.
"Free": Removes risk and feels like a win, making offers irresistible, like "Buy one, get one free."

8. Why do higher prices sometimes mean better quality?

People often assume expensive items are better, especially in areas like wine, electronics, or luxury goods. This is called the "price-quality heuristic."

9. When should brands use high prices?

High prices work for luxury or premium brands aiming for exclusivity. But brands focused on affordability need to keep prices competitive for their audience.

Chapter 10: Consumer Journey Mapping and Touchpoints

1. What is a customer journey?

A customer journey is the full experience a person has with a brand, from first hearing about it to after they've bought something. It includes steps like learning about the product, deciding to buy, and staying connected after the purchase.

2. Why does mapping the customer journey matter?

Mapping helps brands understand what customers need at each step. This way, they can make interactions smoother, improve satisfaction, and build loyalty.

3. What are psychology-based touchpoints?

Psychology-based touchpoints are moments in the journey where brands use psychological principles, like showing reviews (social proof) or offering limited-time deals (scarcity), to connect with customers and motivate them.

4. Can you give examples of touchpoints?

Awareness: Ads with great visuals or stories that grab attention.
Consideration: Reviews and testimonials to build trust.
Decision: Scarcity messages, like "Only 2 left!" to encourage action.
Post-purchase: Personalized follow-ups or thank-you emails to show appreciation.

5. Why is customer experience important at each step?

A great experience keeps customers moving through the journey and builds trust. A bad experience, like a hard-to-use website, can make them leave.

6. How can brands create a positive experience?

Brands can create a positive experience by keeping things consistent and clear. For example, make websites easy to navigate, provide detailed product info, and offer friendly customer support.

7. How do emotions affect the customer journey?

Emotions guide decisions. Excitement might draw someone in, while reassurance during checkout can ease nervousness. Positive emotions keep the journey smooth and memorable.

8. How can brands manage emotions?

Brands can manage emotions by understanding where customers might feel unsure or excited. For example, during purchase, offer satisfaction guarantees to ease worry. After buying, send a thank-you message to keep the excitement alive.

9. What makes a customer journey memorable?

Exceeding expectations! Surprise rewards, helpful service, and personalized touches make customers feel special and more likely to return.

10. How can brands build loyalty?

Brands can build loyalty by:

Loyalty programs: Offer rewards for repeat purchases.
Personalization: Tailor recommendations or emails to the customer.
Quick support: Solve problems fast to build trust.
Exclusive perks: Give early access to products or special events.

By showing customers they're valued, brands can turn one-time buyers into loyal fans.

Chapter 11: Behavioral Economics and Choice Architecture

1. What is behavioral economics?

Behavioral economics studies how emotions and biases affect the way people make decisions. It explains why people don't always act logically, like choosing a pricier product or delaying a decision.

2. How does behavioral economics help marketers?

Behavioral economics helps marketers create strategies that match how people actually think and behave, like using simple offers or emphasizing savings to guide decisions.

3.a. What is choice architecture?

Choice architecture is how options are presented to make decisions easier. For example, showing a few top picks first helps customers focus without feeling overwhelmed.

3.b. Can you give more examples?

Defaults: Pre-selecting options, like auto-renew subscriptions.
Limited options: Offering fewer choices to prevent decision fatigue.
Order of presentation: Highlighting the most popular or recommended items.

4. What are default options, and why do they work?

Default options are pre-set choices, like signing up for auto-renew by default. They work because people often stick with the default due to convenience or trust.

5. Why are default options so effective?

People prefer to avoid change (status quo bias) and like when decisions are made simple. Defaults guide customers while reducing the mental effort needed to decide.

6. What are nudges, and how do they help in marketing?

Nudges are small cues that encourage helpful decisions without limiting choice. For example, showing "Best Seller" on a product gently steers people to consider it.

7. How can brands nudge customers ethically?

Sending reminders: Like emails for abandoned carts.
Personalizing suggestions: Recommend items based on past purchases.
Highlighting benefits: Show perks like "Free shipping with this option."

These approaches help customers make informed choices without feeling pressured.

8.a. What is the paradox of choice?

The paradox of choice says too many options can overwhelm people, making it harder to decide or causing them to give up.

8.b. How can brands fix this?

Brands can fix this by:

Curating options: Offer a smaller, focused selection.
Using filters: Help customers sort items by categories like "Best Sellers."
Adding decision aids: Tools like quizzes or comparisons make choosing simpler.

By reducing overload, brands make shopping easier and more enjoyable.

Chapter 12: Long-Term Customer Relationships and Retention

1. Why is keeping customers as important as finding new ones?

Keeping customers costs less than finding new ones and builds stable revenue. Loyal customers often spend more, return often, and recommend the brand to others, creating a cycle of growth through word-of-mouth.

2. How does loyalty help a brand succeed?

Loyal customers provide steady income, reduce the need for constant advertising, and stick with the brand during tough times. They're also more likely to choose the brand over competitors.

3. What psychological factors build loyalty?

Trust, satisfaction, and belonging. When brands reward loyalty, deliver consistent quality, and connect emotionally with customers, it strengthens their relationship.

4. How do brands use psychology to keep customers loyal?

Brands use psychology to keep customers loyal in the following ways:

Loyalty programs reward repeat buyers.
Personalized messages, like birthday discounts, make customers feel special.
Community-building, like Apple's fan culture, creates a sense of belonging.

5. Why is customer satisfaction important for retention?

Happy and satisfied customers are more likely to stay and recommend the brand. Dissatisfied ones are quick to leave and find alternatives.

6. How can brands improve satisfaction?

To improve satisfaction, brands can ask for feedback through surveys or Net Promoter Scores (NPS). Fix problems quickly and listen to customer concerns to show they're valued.

7. Why is personalization key to loyalty?

Personalization makes customers feel recognized and valued. Tailored offers, messages, and recommendations show the brand cares about their individual needs.

8. What are examples of personalized communication?

Examples of personalized communication are:

Suggesting products based on past purchases.
Sending birthday discounts or anniversary offers.
Tailoring emails to customer interests, like promoting eco-friendly items to someone who values sustainability.

9. What's the difference between loyal customers and advocates?

Loyal customers buy often but don't always promote the brand. Advocates actively recommend and defend the brand, sharing their love with others.

10. How can brands turn customers into advocates?

Brands can turn customers into advocates by:

Offer referral programs with rewards.
Encourage user-generated content, like sharing photos or reviews.
Recognize advocates with exclusive perks, like early access to products or special events.
By making loyal customers feel valued, they're more likely to spread the word and attract new customers.

Chapter 13: Ethics in Marketing Psychology

1. Why is ethics important in marketing psychology?

Ethics ensures that marketing tactics respect customers and don't exploit their subconscious behaviors. Ethical marketing builds trust, leading to stronger, long-term customer relationships.

2. What are ethical boundaries in marketing?

Ethical boundaries involve honesty, transparency, and respecting customer autonomy. For example, it's unethical to use scare tactics or fake claims to sell products.

3. What's the difference between persuasion and manipulation?

Persuasion helps consumers make informed decisions that match their needs, while manipulation uses tricks or pressure to benefit the brand, often at the customer's expense.

4. How can marketers avoid manipulation?

Marketers should avoid practices like:

Fake urgency (e.g., false "limited stock" messages).
Hidden fees.
Fake testimonials or endorsements.
Being upfront and truthful ensures customers trust the brand.

5. What is ethical persuasion, and why does it matter?

Ethical persuasion uses clear, honest communication to guide customers toward choices that genuinely help them. This builds trust and loyalty, benefiting both the customer and the brand.

6. How can marketers practice ethical persuasion?

Marketers can practice ethical persuasion by:

Being transparent about product benefits and costs.
Understanding customer needs and offer relevant solutions.
Using truthful messaging that reflects the product's actual value.

7. What laws protect consumers from unethical marketing?

Laws like the FTC regulations in the U.S. and the EU's Unfair Commercial Practices Directive ensure ads are truthful and transparent, banning deceptive practices.

8. How can marketers comply with these laws?

Marketers can:

Use clear, honest language.
Disclose sponsored content or affiliate links.
Provide evidence for all claims, like product benefits or features.

9. How has data-driven marketing changed ethical considerations?

With access to more personal data, marketers must balance personalization with respect for privacy and consent. Misusing data can harm trust and lead to legal issues.

10. How can brands use data ethically?

Brands can use data ethically by:

Getting clear consent before collecting data.
Allowing customers to control their data (e.g., view or delete it).
Protecting data with strong security measures and avoid sharing it without permission.

By being transparent and respectful, brands can build trust while staying compliant with privacy laws.

Chapter 14: Future Trends in Marketing Psychology

1. What role does artificial intelligence (AI) play in modern marketing?

AI is transforming marketing by enabling more personalized, predictive, and efficient strategies. From chatbots that provide instant customer support to algorithms that recommend products based on browsing history, AI allows brands to create customized experiences at scale. By analyzing vast amounts of data, AI can identify patterns in consumer behavior, preferences, and purchasing habits, helping marketers target consumers with messages that are more relevant and timely.

2. What are some examples of AI-driven marketing tools?

Common AI applications in marketing include:

Predictive analytics: Anticipating consumer needs and behavior based on past actions.
Chatbots: Providing immediate, 24/7 assistance for common customer inquiries.
Dynamic pricing: Adjusting prices in real time based on demand, competition, and consumer behavior.
Recommendation engines: Suggesting products or content tailored to individual preferences. AI not only enhances efficiency but also deepens the brand-consumer connection by delivering highly relevant, timely experiences.

3. How are AR and VR being used in marketing?

AR and VR offer immersive, interactive experiences that help consumers engage with products in new ways. Augmented reality overlays digital information onto the physical world, while virtual reality creates entirely digital environments. Both technologies allow customers to "try before they buy," which can reduce hesitation, increase satisfaction, and drive conversions, especially for products that benefit from visualization, like furniture, fashion, or makeup.

3. Can you give examples of AR and VR applications in marketing?

Here are some popular applications:

Virtual try-ons: Beauty brands like Sephora allow customers to "try on" makeup through AR apps.
Home visualization: IKEA's AR app lets users see how furniture would look in their own rooms.
VR showrooms: Automotive brands create virtual showrooms for customers to examine cars in detail. By making the shopping experience more interactive and personalized, AR and VR increase consumer confidence and engagement, making them powerful tools in marketing's future.

4. What is conscious consumerism, and why is it growing?

Conscious consumerism is when people choose products based on social, environmental, and ethical values. More shoppers care about sustainability, fair trade, and responsible brands, pushing companies to act transparently and align with these values.

5. How are brands responding to conscious consumers?

Brands are:

Using sustainable packaging to reduce waste.
Supporting social causes, like donating sales to charity.
Sharing sourcing details to show ethical practices.
Authenticity is key, shoppers will call out brands for "greenwashing" or fake efforts.

6. How is personalization changing in marketing?

Personalization is becoming smarter and more intuitive, thanks to AI and data. Brands now predict what people want before they ask, personalizing not just recommendations but timing and channels for interaction.

7. What's the future of predictive marketing?

The future of predictive marketing may include:

Anticipatory shipping: Sending items before they're ordered based on past behavior.
Proactive customer service: Fixing problems before customers report them.
Real-time personalization: Changing website layouts or suggestions based on live browsing.
Ethical data handling will be crucial for customer trust in these advances.

8. Why is privacy a bigger concern in marketing?

Privacy is a bigger concern in marketing because, with more data being collected, customers worry about how it's used. Laws like GDPR and CCPA require brands to be clear about data practices, giving people more control over their information.

9. How can brands handle privacy responsibly?

Brands can handle privacy responsibly by:

Being transparent: Explain how data is used and why it helps the customer.
Giving control: Let users easily opt out or adjust preferences.
Using privacy-first tools: Analyze trends without tracking individuals.

Prioritizing privacy earns trust, making customers more willing to share data for better experiences.

Conclusion

To wrap up, understanding how people think, feel, and act is key to building strong connections with customers. This book has shown how psychological ideas can help create better marketing strategies that connect with people, build trust, and grow loyalty.

Knowing what drives decisions helps brands design campaigns that reach their audience and keep them engaged. Being honest and caring in marketing builds strong relationships, and loyal customers not only keep coming back but also share positive experiences with others. As technology and customer needs change, brands must stay updated with trends like AI and sustainable choices while remaining ethical. Personalizing customer experiences is powerful, but it's important to respect privacy and build trust when using data.

By applying these ideas responsibly, brands can create meaningful experiences that customers remember and value. The future of marketing lies in truly understanding people and creating connections that last. Use what you've learned here to grow your business and improve how people experience your brand. Thank you for joining this journey into marketing psychology!

www.ingramcontent.com/pod-product-compliance
Lightning Source LLC
Chambersburg PA
CBHW070943220526
45469CB00007B/2497